Pebble® Plus

EXPLORE LIFE CYCLES

A Sunflower's Life Cycle

by Mary R. Dunn

T0050909

CAPSTONE PRESS
a capstone imprint

Pebble Plus is published by Capstone Press,
1710 Roe Crest Drive, North Mankato, Minnesota 56003
www.mycapstone.com

Copyright © 2018 by Capstone Press, a Capstone imprint. All rights reserved. No part of this publication may be reproduced in whole or in part, or stored in a retrieval system, or transmitted in any form or by any means, electronic, mechanical, photocopying, recording, or otherwise, without written permission of the publisher.

Library of Congress Cataloging-in-Publication Data
Library of Congress Cataloging-in-Publication data is available on the Library of Congress website.
ISBN 978-1-5157-7050-3 (library binding)
ISBN 978-1-5157-7056-5 (paperback)
ISBN 978-1-5157-7062-6 (eBook PDF)

Editorial Credits
Anna Butzer, editor; Kyle Grenz, designer
Wanda Winch, media researcher; Kathy McColley, production specialist

Photo Credits
Shutterstock: AMC Images, 1, Bogdan Wankowicz, 5, 7, boyphare, 19, dimid_86, 21, Emilio100, 9, Helen's Photos, 15, Jerry Lin, 11, Narudom Chaisuwon, cover, NattapolStudiO, 17, Samiran Sarker, sunflower silhouette, SJ Travel Photo and Video, back cover, Yuthana Choradet, 13

Note to Parents and Teachers

The Explore Life Cycles set supports national science standards related to life science. This book describes and illustrates the life cycle of apple trees. The images support early readers in understanding the text. The repetition of words and phrases helps early readers learn new words. This book also introduces early readers to subject-specific vocabulary words, which are defined in the Glossary section. Early readers may need assistance to read some words and to use the Table of Contents, Glossary, Read More, Internet Sites, Critical Thinking Questions, and Index sections of the book.

Table of Contents

A Flower Seed

Pop! Under the warm spring soil

a seed breaks open.

It will grow to be a tall plant

with yellow flowers.

It is a sunflower seed.

4

The seed sends out roots.

Roots push deep into the soil.

They take in water and minerals.

A green shoot pokes out of the dirt.

Sprouting Leaves

The shoot becomes the plant's stem.

The first leaves sprout from the stem.

Leaves use water, sunlight, and air

to make food for the plant.

Tiny hairs cover the stem.

The hairs stop insects from climbing

up the stem and eating the leaves.

More leaves grow on the stem.

Growing Tall

The stem grows taller and taller.

Some may grow over

12 feet (3 meters) high. Wow!

Green leaves called bracts

form on the flower bud.

13

As the bracts unfold, yellow
flower petals poke out.
The petals open and the
flower head grows bigger.

Blooming Flowers

Sunflower heads have

hundreds of tiny florets.

Florets are covered with pollen dust.

Bees land on the bright florets.

Bees land on many sunflowers, spreading pollen among the florets. Florets have tiny ovules.

Pollen and ovules form new seeds.

In the fall some sunflower seeds
are harvested. Other seeds fall
to the ground. They will grow
into new plants in spring.

GLOSSARY

bract—part of a plant that protects the bud while it grows

floret—tiny flower that is part of a flower head

flower head—flower that is made up of many tiny florets

harvest—to gather ripe crops

mineral—chemical that plants need to stay healthy

ovule—female egg that joins with male pollen to form a seed

petal—a small colorful part of a flower

pollen—tiny male parts of a plant

root—part of a plant that grows under the ground and takes in water

shoot—the white stem growing out of a seed that becomes a plant

soil—top layer of ground where plants grow

stem—the part of a plant that connects the roots to the leaves

READ MORE

De la Bedoyere, Camilla. *Seed to Sunflower.* New York: Sandy Creek, 2013.

Jones, Grace. *Life Cycle of a Sunflower.* Norfolk, UK: Booklife, 2016.

Phelps, Bonnie. *The Life Cycle of a Sunflower.* Watch Them Grow! New York: PowerKids Press, 2016.

INTERNET SITES

FactHound offers a safe, fun way to find Internet sites related to this book. All of the sites on FactHound have been researched by our staff.

Here's all you do:

Visit *www.facthound.com*

Type in this code: 9781515770503

Check out projects, games and lots more at
www.capstonekids.com

23

CRITICAL THINKING QUESTIONS

1. How do roots help the sunflower to grow?

2. Why is it hard for insects to eat sunflower leaves?

3. Find the word in the glossary that tells where plants grow.

INDEX